Fact Finders®

WE SHALL OVERCOME

THE MARCH ON WASHINGTON

A PRIMARY SOURCE EXPLORATION OF THE PIVOTAL PROTEST

by Heather E. Schwartz

Consultant:
Bruce Allen Murphy, PhD
Fred Morgan Kirby Professor of Civil Rights
Lafayette College
Easton, Pennsylvania

CAPSTONE PRESS
a capstone imprint

Fact Finders Books are published by Capstone Press,
1710 Roe Crest Drive, North Mankato, Minnesota 56003
www.capstonepub.com

Library of Congress Cataloging-in-Publication Data
Schwartz, Heather E.
The March on Washington : a primary source exploration of the pivotal protest / By Heather E. Schwartz.
pages cm. — (Fact finders. We shall overcome.)
Includes bibliographical references and index.
ISBN 978-1-4914-0223-8 (library binding) — ISBN 978-1-4914-0232-0 (pbk.) — ISBN 978-1-4914-0228-3 (ebook pdf)
1. March on Washington for Jobs and Freedom (1963 : Washington, D.C.)—Sources—Juvenile literature . 2. Civil
rights demonstrations—Washington (D.C.)—History—20th century—Sources—Juvenile literature. 3. African
Americans—Civil rights—History—Sources—Juvenile literature. 4. King, Martin Luther, Jr., 1929-1968—Juvenile
literature. I. Title.
F200.S39 2014
975.3′041—dc23   2014005458

Summary: Uses primary sources to tell the story of the March on Washington during the U.S. civil rights movement.

Editorial Credits
Jennifer Besel, editor; Cynthia Akiyoshi, designer; Wanda Winch, media researcher;
     Charmaine Whitman, production specialist

Photo Credits
AP Images, 6, 10, 17; Corbis: Bettmann, 28, Bob Adelman, 21; Courtesy of Arkansas Democrat-Gazette, cover
(bkgrnd), 25; Getty Images Inc: Bob Parent, 19, Time Life Pictures/Francis Miller, 26; The John F. Kennedy
Presidential Library and Museum, 12; Library of Congress: Prints and Photographs Division, 5, 9, 11, 13, 15, 23;
Lyndon B. Johnson Library: Yoichi Okamoto, 27; National Archives and Records Administration, 16; Newscom:
Getty Images Inc/AFP, cover, 29; Shutterstock: Olga k, paper background, Picsfive, paper pieces; Special Collections,
University of Memphis Libraries, 7

Printed in the United States of America in Stevens Point, Wisconsin.
032014   008092WZF14

TABLE OF CONTENTS

A NOTE ABOUT PRIMARY SOURCES

Primary sources are newspaper articles, photographs, speeches, or other documents that were created during an event. They are great ways to see how people spoke and felt during that time. You'll find primary sources from the time of the March on Washington throughout this book. Within the text, primary source quotations are colored blue and set in italic type.

Chapter One

A MARCH FOR CHANGE

Almost 300,000 people stood on the lawn in front of the Lincoln Memorial in Washington, D.C. The crowd was outraged and angry, but it was peaceful and calm. No one raised a fist or threw a punch. Instead they poured their feelings out in passionate songs and powerful words.

"We are tired. We are tired of being beaten by policemen. We are tired of seeing our people locked up in jail over and over again. And then you holler, 'Be patient.' How long can we be patient? We want our freedom, and we want it now!"

The crowd was a mix of people, black and white. Their skin-deep differences were obvious. But their passion for equality united them. They wanted change that would give black Americans their full rights as citizens.

"... By the forces of our demands, our determination, and our numbers, we shall splinter the **segregated** *South into a thousand pieces and put them together in an image of God and democracy."*

—John Lewis, a civil rights leader at the march

segregate—to keep people of different races apart in schools and other public places

> ▶ Photographer Warren K. Leffler captured the scene of thousands of civil rights supporters filling the Washington Mall from the Lincoln Memorial to the Washington Monument.

On August 28, 1963, that crowd created the largest nonviolent protest the country had ever seen. The March on Washington for Jobs and Freedom brought nationwide attention to the civil rights movement.

FACT

John Lewis was a major leader in the civil rights movement. About 20 years after the march, he was elected to Congress.

Chapter Two

PLANNING A PROTEST

The March on Washington was organized to protest **discrimination** and segregation laws that ruled the South. In southern states, African-Americans and whites went to separate schools. They sat in separate areas of restaurants. When they rode buses, they sat in separate sections.

Many white Southerners believed segregation was their right. They felt they should be free to decide if blacks and whites would live together. Alabama Governor George Wallace said, *"Let us rise to the call for freedom-loving blood that is in us and send our answer to the tyranny that clanks its chains upon the South ... I say segregation now, segregation tomorrow, segregation forever."*

► Many students protested against integrating schools. These three students picketed outside their school in Clinton, Tennessee, on August 27, 1956.

discrimination—treating people unfairly because of their race, country of birth, or gender

African-Americans tried to register to vote throughout the South. But many were turned away because they couldn't pass the unfair tests.

African-Americans and many white people did not agree that segregation was a right. They began protesting the laws by disobeying segregation rules. It wasn't easy to change the laws, however. African-Americans didn't have voting power to elect officials to end segregation. Southern states had created laws to prevent them from voting. *"... You had to pass a so-called literacy test, pay a poll tax. On one occasion, a man was asked to count the number of bubbles on a bar of soap. On another occasion, one was asked to count the number of jelly beans in a jar—all to keep them from casting their ballot,"* recalled John Lewis.

A Growing Nonviolent Movement

By the 1950s African-Americans had begun organizing nonviolent protests against segregation. In many cases protesters simply sat in "white" sections of restaurants and buses. *"You go to a counter. You do not request that the person sitting next to you get up and leave. You merely come in and sit down beside him ... You cause no violence ..."* explained one activist at a sit-in in Nashville. Soon these nonviolent protests swept through the South.

The protests brought attention to the segregation problem. But black Americans were still struggling. In 1962 A. Philip Randolph felt it was time for a nonviolent protest that would capture the attention of America's leaders. He wanted a huge march on Washington.

Randolph knew the civil rights movement's major leaders had to be involved in a protest of this size. The leaders came from organizations with different ideas about what mattered most. Eventually they decided the protest would be called the March on Washington for Jobs and Freedom. It would focus on asking the government to pass laws protecting all Americans' rights, including the right to vote. They also wanted the government to stop discrimination in the workplace.

The Organizers

The civil rights leaders Randolph pulled together were often called the "Big Six" by the press.

| John Lewis | Whitney Young Jr. | A. Philip Randolph | Rev. Dr. Martin Luther King Jr. | James Farmer | Roy Wilkins |

John Lewis—chairman of the Student Nonviolent Coordinating Committee

Whitney Young Jr.—executive director of the National Urban League

A. Philip Randolph—president of the Brotherhood of Sleeping Car Porters, a labor union that organized African-American railroad workers

Rev. Dr. Martin Luther King Jr.—president and founding member of the Southern Christian Leadership Conference

James Farmer—cofounder of the Congress of Racial Equality (CORE)

Roy Wilkins—executive secretary of the National Association for the Advancement of Colored People (NAACP)

Putting It Together

Randolph's friend Bayard Rustin was put in charge of planning the March on Washington. From a small office in Harlem, New York, he and his staff spread the word about the march. They organized transportation for marchers. They made sure marchers would have food, water, restrooms, and medical care. Every detail was up to them.

"We march to redress old grievances and to help resolve an American crisis," read an organizing manual for the event. *"We march to demonstrate, massively and dramatically, our unalterable opposition to these forces ... Jobs and Freedom are needed NOW."*

► Bayard Rustin (left), along with other march leaders, gave interviews to spread the word about the event. Rustin originally planned for 100,000 people to march on Washington.

FACT

Rustin had just two months to plan the march. With 200 volunteers helping, Rustin put together one of the largest peaceful protests in U.S. history.

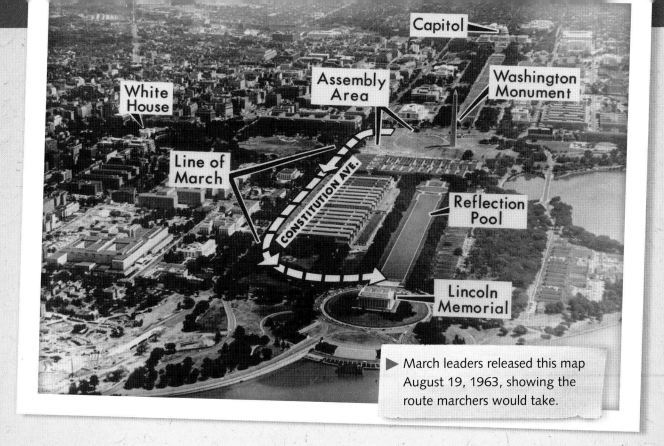

March leaders released this map August 19, 1963, showing the route marchers would take.

The First March

The 1963 march wasn't a new idea. Randolph and Rustin had planned a similar event more than 20 years earlier. During the 1940s thousands of Americans were finding jobs in the defense industry. They were preparing the United States for World War II (1939–1945). But employers refused to hire African-Americans for most jobs.

To protest the discrimination, Randolph and Rustin organized a March on Washington in 1941. They expected more than 100,000 marchers. The idea scared white leaders so much that U.S. President Franklin Roosevelt took action. He issued an order banning discrimination based on race in the defense industry. After this victory the 1941 march was canceled.

Against the March

Not everyone believed a mass protest was a good idea. President John F. Kennedy had been working to gain support for his Civil Rights Act. The law was meant to protect black Americans' rights. Kennedy feared the march would become violent. And if that happened Congress members might not support the act. Kennedy told the organizers, *"We want success in the Congress, not just a big show at the Capitol."*

▶ President John F. Kennedy

▶ Malcolm X

Malcolm X was a black leader with the opposite concern. He worried the march would not become violent. Unlike civil rights leaders, Malcolm X encouraged followers to use violence when necessary.

"... the black people in this country have been the victims of violence at the hands of the white man for 400 years ... when it comes to defending himself, black people ... should have the right to defend ourselves also."

FACT

The fear of violence was so great that 4,000 army soldiers were stationed around Washington, D.C., during the march. Another 15,000 paratroopers were ready to move in if needed. Rustin also trained almost 2,000 people to serve as parade marshals.

Chapter Three
A HISTORIC DAY

The opposition couldn't stop those who believed in the march. On the morning of August 28, 1963, thousands of marchers gathered at the Washington Monument. *"Hundreds and thousands of Americans came together. Blacks, whites, Latinos, Asian Americans, Native Americans, men, women, children,"* recalled John Lewis.

People began singing freedom songs. Then the crowd started to move as one down Constitution and Independence Avenues. More people joined in as the marchers peacefully moved toward the Lincoln Memorial. The numbers swelled to almost 300,000 marchers. Strangers held hands and sang "We Shall Overcome." *"We shall overcome … We'll walk hand in hand some day … We shall all be free some day … We shall overcome …"*

FACT

More than 2,000 buses and 21 trains filled with people arrived in Washington, D.C., the morning of August 28, 1963. Thousands more people arrived by plane and car.

▶ Marchers carrying signs filled Constitution Avenue in Washington, D.C., during the event.

At the Lincoln Memorial, marchers gathered to hear leaders speak in the afternoon. People filled every space on the National Mall. Fanning themselves in the heat, they were moved by Randolph's opening speech.

"We're gathered here for the longest demonstration in the history of this nation. Let the nation and the world know the meaning of our numbers. We are not a pressure group. We are not an organization or a group of organizations. We are not a mob. We are the advanced guard of a massive, moral revolution for jobs and freedom."

▶ the official program for the March on Washington

MARCH ON WASHINGTON FOR JOBS AND FREEDOM
AUGUST 28, 1963

LINCOLN MEMORIAL PROGRAM

1.	The National Anthem	Led by Marian Anderson.
2.	Invocation	The Very Rev. Patrick O'Boyle, *Archbishop of Washington.*
3.	Opening Remarks	A. Philip Randolph, *Director March on Washington for Jobs and Freedom.*
4.	Remarks	Dr. Eugene Carson Blake, *Stated Clerk, United Presbyterian Church of the U.S.A.; Vice Chairman, Commission on Race Relations of the National Council of Churches of Christ in America.*
5.	Tribute to Negro Women Fighters for Freedom Daisy Bates Diane Nash Bevel Mrs. Medgar Evers Mrs. Herbert Lee Rosa Parks Gloria Richardson	Mrs. Medgar Evers
6.	Remarks	John Lewis, *National Chairman, Student Nonviolent Coordinating Committee.*
7.	Remarks	Walter Reuther, *President, United Automobile, Aerospace and Agricultural Implement Wokers of America, AFL-CIO; Chairman, Industrial Union Department, AFL-CIO.*
8.	Remarks	James Farmer, *National Director, Congress of Racial Equality.*
9.	Selection	Eva Jessye Choir
10.	Prayer	Rabbi Uri Miller, *President Synagogue Council of America.*
11.	Remarks	Whitney M. Young, Jr., *Executive Director, National Urban League.*
12.	Remarks	Mathew Ahmann, *Executive Director, National Catholic Conference for Interracial Justice.*
13.	Remarks	Roy Wilkins, *Executive Secretary, National Association for the Advancement of Colored People.*
14.	Selection	Miss Mahalia Jackson
15.	Remarks	Rabbi Joachim Prinz, *President American Jewish Congress.*
16.	Remarks	The Rev. Dr. Martin Luther King, Jr., *President, Southern Christian Leadership Conference.*
17.	The Pledge	A Philip Randolph
18.	Benediction	Dr. Benjamin E. Mays, *President, Morehouse College.*

"WE SHALL OVERCOME"

A. Philip Randolph gave the opening speech at the Lincoln Memorial.

Songs and Speeches

James Farmer was scheduled to speak later in the day, but he had been jailed for **demonstrating** in Louisiana. He sent his speech to be read. *"We will not slow down, we will not stop our militant, peaceful demonstrations,"* his words assured the crowd. *"We will not come off the streets until we can work at any job **befitting** our skills any place in the land."*

Whitney Young Jr. continued the call to keep marching until black Americans were equal Americans. *"Civil rights, which are God-given and constitutionally guaranteed, are not negotiable in 1963 ... The rumble of the drums of discontent ... are heard in all parts of the world ... Our march is a march for America. It is a march just begun."*

demonstrate—to join together with others to protest something

befit—to be suitable to

When gospel singer Mahalia Jackson sang, she rallied the crowd. The lyrics to "I Been 'Buked and I Been Scorned" spoke of being unappreciated and mistreated.

"I been 'buked and I been scorned ...
I'm gonna tell my Lord when I get home ...
how you been mistreating me so long."

The song had personal meaning to her as the granddaughter of a slave. It rang true to the cheering crowd gathered in Washington, D.C., too.

Mahalia Jackson

"I Have a Dream"

By the time Jackson finished singing, it was late in the day. The marchers were hot and tired. But nothing could dampen their enthusiasm when the Rev. Dr. Martin Luther King Jr. stood to speak. Throughout his speech the crowd clapped and cheered.

"Now is the time to make real the promises of democracy. Now is the time to rise from the dark and desolate valley of segregation to the sunlit path of racial justice ... So even though we face the difficulties of today and tomorrow, I still have a dream ...

"I have a dream that one day this nation will rise up, and live out the true meaning of its creed: 'We hold these truths to be self-evident, that all men are created equal'...

"I have a dream that my four little children will one day live in a nation where they will not be judged by the color of their skin but by the content of their character ...

"I have a dream that one day down in Alabama, with its vicious racists ... one day right there in Alabama little black boys and black girls will be able to join hands with little white boys and white girls as sisters and brothers ..."

He concluded with a cry for freedom: *"From every mountainside, let freedom ring ... When we let it ring ... we will be able to speed up that day when all of God's children ... will be able to join hands and sing ... 'Free at last. Free at last. Thank God almighty. We are free at last!'"*

As King stepped down to a swell of applause, the marchers knew they were making history.

Chapter Four
MARCH AND EFFECT

People watching the march on TV and listening on the radio felt the power in those words too. People were moved, Kennedy included. He was convinced that the peaceful demonstration could help win support for his Civil Rights Act.

When the march ended, Kennedy met with the organizers. Less than two hours later, he issued a statement praising the marchers. He promised the government would help all Americans and legally protect their rights.

"One cannot help but be impressed with the deep fervor and the quiet dignity that characterizes the thousands who have gathered in the Nation's Capital from across the country to demonstrate their faith and confidence in our democratic form of government," he said. *"The executive branch of the Federal Government will continue its efforts to obtain increased employment and to eliminate discrimination in employment practices, two of the prime goals of the March."*

▶ Kennedy (fourth from right) met with march leaders after the successful event.

Moved by King's Words

Fifty years after the march, Yahoo News asked people to share what they remembered of the march. Ronald Franklin was 14 years old when he heard King's speech on TV.

"Listening to Dr. King, I really began to believe that one day I would be judged not on the color of my skin, but on the content of my character," he said. *"The speech planted seeds of hope and confidence that helped me make it through the first non-segregated school I ever attended, the University of Tennessee. And they are still with me today."*

Backlash and Bombing

Others were not convinced the March on Washington was a success. In his autobiography, Malcolm X wrote, *"Yes, I was there. I observed that circus. Who ever heard of angry revolutionists all harmonizing 'We Shall Overcome' … while tripping and swaying along arm-in-arm with the very people they were supposed to be angrily revolting against?"*

The number of people who showed up to march peacefully was proof that the civil rights movement was gaining power. Unfortunately, life would get worse before it got better.

Hate groups grew even more determined to stop African-Americans from gaining equality. Less than one month after the march, a hate group called the Ku Klux Klan (KKK) struck back. They bombed a church in Birmingham, Alabama, killing four African-American girls. *"Dozens of survivors, their faces dripping blood from the glass that flew out of the church's stained glass windows, staggered around the building in a cloud of white dust raised by the explosion,"* read a news report.

The bombing led to more violence. Riots broke out in the streets of Birmingham. White people set black-owned businesses on fire. Black people threw stones at cars owned by whites. Two African-American boys were shot to death by police called in to control the situation.

The *Arkansas Gazette* reported on the violence in Birmingham in September 1963.

FACT

The four KKK members who bombed the church walked free for years. It wasn't until 1977 that one of the men was sent to prison for the attack. Two others were sent to prison in 2001 and 2002. The other bomber died before he was charged.

New Laws

Despite the backlash the march inspired lasting, positive changes. Kennedy's Civil Rights Act gained support. The act was signed into law by President Lyndon Johnson in 1964. The new law banned segregation and employment discrimination. Employers could no longer refuse to hire someone based on race, skin color, national **origin**, religion, or gender.

▶ Protesters from many organizations came to Washington, D.C., to try to persuade lawmakers to vote against the Civil Rights Act.

origin—where someone comes from

Johnson signed the Voting Rights Act on August 6, 1965. Civil rights leaders, including many who worked on the march, were there to see it.

The Civil Rights Act also paved the way for another landmark law. The Voting Rights Act of 1965 protected black Americans' right to vote. Many Southern politicians spoke and voted against the act. Representative James Martin of Alabama said to the House, *"The real American tragedy will be that if the President's proposal is made into law and we turn the ballot box over to those who cannot read, write, or comprehend the responsibility of citizenship, this Republic as we know it will cease to be."*

But eventually, the act was signed into law. Before signing it, Johnson said, *"This Act flows from a clear and simple wrong. Its only purpose is to right that wrong. Millions of Americans are denied the right to vote because of their color. This law will ensure them the right to vote."*

A Lasting Impact

The March on Washington for Jobs and Freedom didn't mark the end of injustice in America. But it did mark the beginning of major change. The march proved that large, peaceful protests could be an effective way to demand new laws. *"The months and years ahead will bring new evidence of masses in motion for freedom,"* Randolph said during the march. *"The March on Washington is not the climax of our struggle, but a new beginning not only for the Negro but for all Americans who thirst for freedom and a better life."*

▶ Johnson signed the Civil Rights Act into law July 2, 1964. But violence against African-Americans continued. Taken on July 21, 1964, this photograph captures the fear of a race riot in Brooklyn, New York.

▶ Black and white leaders joined hands during the March on Washington to show they stood together in their quest for equality.

Selected Bibliography

"Final Plans for the March on Washington for Jobs and Freedom" Organizing Manual No. 2. Online by Civil Rights Movement Veterans. http://www.crmvet.org/docs/moworg2.pdf

"John Lewis at March on Washington." August 28, 1963. Online by CBS News. http://www.dailymotion.com/video/x15ska3#user_search=1

Johnson, Lyndon Baines. "Remarks on the Signing of the Voting Rights Act." August 6, 1975. Online by Miller Center of University of Virginia. http://millercenter.org/president/speeches/detail/4034

Kennedy, John F. "Statement by the President on the March on Washington for Jobs and Freedom," August 28, 1963. Online by Gerhard Peters and John T. Woolley, The American Presidency Project. http://www.presidency.ucsb.edu/ws/?pid=9383

"Mahalia Jackson Wows Crowd at March on Washington." August 28, 1963. Online by CBS News. http://www.dailymotion.com/video/x15sk9o_mahalia-jackson-wows-crowd-at-march-on-washington_news

Malcolm X interview. "Citizen King: Three Perspectives." American Experience. http://www.pbs.org/wgbh/amex/mlk/sfeature/sf_video_pop_03_qt.html

"The March on Washington." National Archives and Records Administration. https://archive.org/details/gov.archives.arc.49737

"The March on Washington Video Part 2." Eyes on the Prize: America's Civil Rights Movement 1954–1985. http://www.pbs.org/wgbh/amex/eyesontheprize/story/08_washington.html

Martin, James. "The Real American Tragedy." March 15, 1965. Congressional Record—House. http://www.archives.gov/legislative/resources/education/voting-rights/images/facsimiles-all.pdf

Young, Whitney Jr. "March for Jobs and Freedom." August 28, 1963. Online by History and Politics Out Loud. https://soundcloud.com/hpol/whitney-young-jr-speech-march

Glossary

befit (be-FIT)—to be suitable to or proper for

demonstrate (DEM-uhn-strate)—to join together with others to protest something

discrimination (dis-kri-muh-NAY-shuhn)—treating people unfairly because of their race, country of birth, or gender

origin (OR-uh-jin)—where someone or something comes from

segregate (SEG-ruh-gate)—to keep people of different races apart in schools and other public places

Critical Thinking Using the Common Core

1. Speakers at the March on Washington program spoke in front of the statue of Abraham Lincoln. Why was this backdrop important? Use other resources and this text to defend your answer. (Integration of Knowledge and Ideas)

2. Compare the excerpt of Martin Luther King Jr.'s speech on page 20 with the quotation from Malcolm X on page 13. What action words does each speaker use? How do those action words shape the tone of each message? (Craft and Structure)

Internet Sites

FactHound offers a safe, fun way to find Internet sites related to this book. All of the sites on FactHound have been researched by our staff.

Here's all you do:
Visit *www.facthound.com*
Type in this code: 9781491402238

 Check out projects, games and lots more at **www.capstonekids.com**

Index